21st Century Disasters

California Wildfires

by Sue Gagliardi

FOCUS READERS

BEACON

www.focusreaders.com

Focus Readers is distributed by North Star Editions:
sales@northstareditions.com | 888-417-0195

Produced for Focus Readers by Red Line Editorial.

Photographs ©: Francis Specker/AP Images, cover, 1; Noah Berger/AP Images, 4, 7, 21, 22, 24; Red Line Editorial, 8; Krista Kennell/Shutterstock Images, 10; Glevalex/Shutterstock Images, 13; Digital Media Pro/Shutterstock Images, 15, 29; Kay Prinsloo/Shutterstock Images, 16–17; John Locher/AP Images, 18; FCG/Shutterstock Images, 26

Library of Congress Cataloging-in-Publication Data
Names: Gagliardi, Sue, 1969- author.
Title: California wildfires / by Sue Gagliardi.
Description: Lake Elmo, MN : Focus Readers, [2020] | Series: 21st century disasters | Audience: Grade 4 to 6. | Includes bibliographical references and index.
Identifiers: LCCN 2019010455 (print) | LCCN 2019011981 (ebook) | ISBN 9781641859431 (pdf) | ISBN 9781641858748 (ebook) | ISBN 9781641857369 (hardcover) | ISBN 9781641858052 (pbk.)
Subjects: LCSH: Wildfires--California--Juvenile literature.
Classification: LCC SD421.23 (ebook) | LCC SD421.23 .G34 2020 (print) | DDC 634.9/61809794--dc23
LC record available at https://lccn.loc.gov/2019010455

Printed in the United States of America
Mankato, MN
May, 2019

About the Author

Sue Gagliardi writes fiction, nonfiction, and poetry for children. Her books include *Fairies*, *Get Outside in Winter*, and *Get Outside in Spring*. Her work appears in children's magazines including *Highlights Hello*, *Highlights High Five*, *Ladybug*, and *Spider*. She teaches kindergarten and lives in Pennsylvania with her husband and son.

Table of Contents

CHAPTER 1

Raging Flames 5

CHAPTER 2

Understanding Wildfires 11

Wildfires 16

CHAPTER 3

Survivor Stories 19

CHAPTER 4

After the Blaze 25

Focus on California Wildfires • 28

Glossary • 30

To Learn More • 31

Index • 32

Chapter 1

Raging Flames

Smoke filled the air in Paradise, California. Mary Gowins and her family looked out their window. It was 10:30 a.m. But the sky was as dark as midnight. The town was about to face a wildfire.

A wildfire burns down a home in Paradise, California.

The wildfire had started in a nearby forest. The flames grew quickly. Burning **embers** flew all around. Many houses caught on fire. Firefighters tried to battle the blaze. But it kept burning. Bits of ash fell like snow.

People in Paradise had to **evacuate**. Mary and her family grabbed a few things to take with them. Then they tried to drive to safety. So did thousands of other people. Their cars filled the

Tens of thousands of people in California fled the huge wildfire by car.

narrow mountain roads. Traffic jams formed. Meanwhile, the fire kept spreading. As it raced toward them, many people left their cars.

OTHER CALIFORNIA WILDFIRES

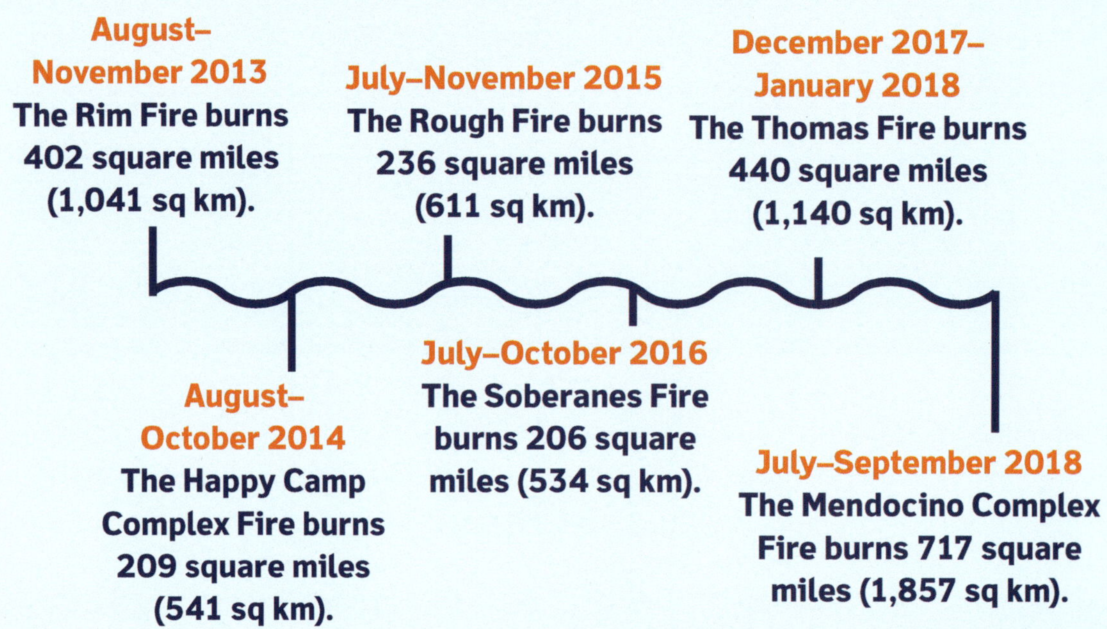

They ran as fast as they could to escape the flames.

The wildfire was called the Camp Fire. It began on November 8, 2018. By the next day, 52,000 people had to evacuate nearby towns. And the fire kept growing.

California has had many wildfires. The Camp Fire was not the biggest. But it was the deadliest one yet. The Camp Fire raged in northern California for 17 days. It burned 239 square miles (620 sq km) of land. More than 85 people died.

A megafire is a wildfire that burns more than 156 square miles (405 sq km).

Chapter 2

Understanding Wildfires

Wildfires are large fires that spread quickly through bushes, grass, or trees. Like all fires, they need heat, **fuel**, and **oxygen** to burn. Sometimes, a wildfire starts when lightning strikes the ground.

A wildfire's flames send thick smoke into the air.

But humans cause most wildfires. In fact, people start more than 90 percent of wildfires in California.

People may be careless with matches. Or they may leave campfires unattended. These small fires can spread. When a fire gets

Wildfires are also known as forest fires, bush fires, or brush fires. These names are based on what the fires burn.

Leaving campfires unwatched can cause wildfires.

too big to control, it becomes a wildfire.

Wildfires often happen during hot, dry weather. Heat and **drought** make the forest dry. Dry plants can catch fire more easily. Even a small spark can grow into a wildfire.

Wind increases the risk for wildfires. For example, the Santa Ana winds are hot and dry. They come from the mountains of Southern California. The winds dry the trees and grass. This dry fuel helps the fire burn.

A large wildfire can create strong winds. The winds can blow 120 miles per hour (193 km/h).

Firefighters use helicopters to fight forest fires.

Wind also helps wildfires spread. Wind brings more oxygen to the flames. Adding oxygen helps a fire grow. In addition, wind can carry embers long distances from the fire. The embers spread the fire to new places when they fall.

Wildfires

Wildfires spread quickly. People who live in areas where they are common must be ready to leave right away. Families should practice an evacuation plan. And people should prepare an emergency kit. They should pack clothing, food, and water. The kit should also hold **first aid** supplies.

People can work to protect their homes, too. They can clear away plants and **debris** near the house. That way, the fire will have fewer things to burn. It will not spread as quickly. Water from pools and sprinklers can also help slow the fire.

Fires can only spread to places with fuel to burn.

Paradise
Elementary
School Rules
Be Safe
Be Respectful
Be Responsible

Chapter 3

Survivor Stories

The Camp Fire began as a small brush fire. On November 8, it burned in Butte County, California. Paradise Elementary School was 15 miles (24 km) away. Its teachers and students needed to evacuate.

The Camp Fire destroyed Paradise Elementary School.

Parents came to get most students. But four students were still at the school as the fire drew near. Two teachers drove them to safety.

Some people couldn't drive away from the fire. One was Nichole Jolly. Her car filled with smoke. Flames surrounded it. Nichole left her car and started to run.

Soon she reached a fire truck. The firefighters picked her up. They gave her a **fire blanket** for protection from the heat. But the

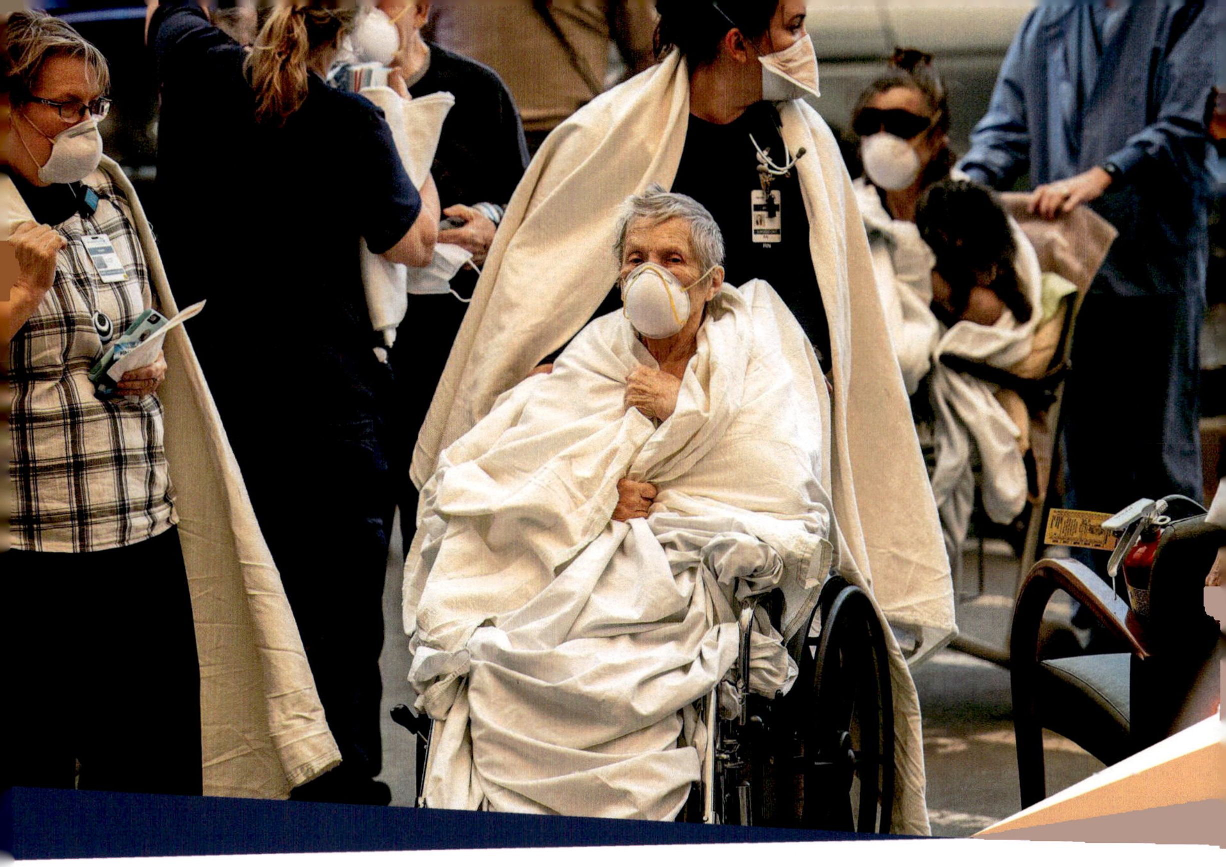

People evacuate a hospital in Paradise, California.

truck was stuck. It had no clear path to drive away from the flames.

A bulldozer came and cleared a path. Then the fire truck drove to the hospital where Nichole worked.

Firefighters battle the Camp Fire.

She and the other nurses helped keep the patients safe.

Firefighters rushed to California from around the United States.

They worked together to stop the fire. One group sent an airplane called the Global SuperTanker. This firefighting plane dumped water on the flames from above. On November 21, heavy rains began to slow the fire. By November 25, the Camp Fire was under control.

The Global SuperTanker is the largest firefighting plane in the world. It can carry 20,000 gallons (76,000 liters) of water.

Chapter 4

After the Blaze

After a wildfire, **relief** groups come to the area. Some groups provide food, clothing, and shelter for people who have lost their homes. Other groups help rebuild. It can take years for an area to recover.

This firebreak runs through a forest.

To prevent future damage, people create firebreaks. A firebreak is an area where people have cleared away fuel. For example, people may cut tall grass. Without fuel, a wildfire can't spread. Sometimes, people start controlled burns.

These fires stay within a certain area. They burn fuel before a wildfire can.

However, wildfires are not all bad. They remove dead plants so new plants can grow. They keep insect numbers under control. In fact, occasional wildfires help keep the forest healthy.

Some evergreen trees release seeds only during wildfires.

FOCUS ON

California Wildfires

Write your answers on a separate piece of paper.

1. Write a paragraph describing how wind affects wildfires.
2. Do you think controlled burns are a good way to prevent wildfires? Why or why not?
3. What three things are needed for a fire to burn?
   - **A.** heat, fuel, and oxygen
   - **B.** embers, smoke, and water
   - **C.** air, wind, and drought
4. What might happen in an area where wildfires never happen?
   - **A.** The forest would be healthier and taller.
   - **B.** The number of insects would increase too quickly.
   - **C.** New plants would be able to grow more easily.

5. What does **unattended** mean in this book?

*People may be careless with matches. Or they may leave campfires **unattended**.*

A. not watched
B. not started
C. not planned

6. What does **controlled** mean in this book?

*Sometimes, people start **controlled** burns. These fires stay within a certain area.*

A. made by accident
B. kept within limits
C. set completely free

Answer key on page 32.

Glossary

debris
The remains of something broken.

drought
A long period of little or no rain.

embers
Small, hot pieces of fuel from a fire. Most embers have no flames, but they still burn or glow.

evacuate
To leave a place of danger.

fire blanket
A sheet of material that will not burn. It can be placed over a small fire to put it out.

first aid
Things that are used for helping sick or injured people.

fuel
Material that burns to create heat.

oxygen
A gas in the air that humans and animals need to breathe and that fires need to burn.

relief
Help for people in need.

To Learn More

BOOKS

Furgang, Kathy. *Wildfires*. Washington, DC: National Geographic, 2015.

Raum, Elizabeth. *Wildfire!* Mankato, MN: Amicus, 2017.

Westmark, Jon. *Smoke Jumpers in Action*. Mankato, MN: The Child's World, 2017.

NOTE TO EDUCATORS

Visit **www.focusreaders.com** to find lesson plans, activities, links, and other resources related to this title.

Index

B

brush fire, 12, 19
bush fire, 12

C

Camp Fire, 8–9, 19, 23

D

drought, 13

E

embers, 6, 15
evacuate, 6, 9, 19

F

firebreak, 26
firefighters, 6, 20, 22–23
forest fire, 12
fuel, 11, 14, 26–27

G

Global SuperTanker, 23

P

Paradise, California, 5–6

S

smoke, 5, 20

W

water, 16, 23
wind, 14–15

Answer Key: 1. Answers will vary; **2.** Answers will vary; **3.** A; **4.** B; **5.** A; **6.** B